Data Analytics

Insiders Guide to Master Data Analytics

from various sources. Please consult a licensed professional before attempting any techniques outlined in this book.

By reading this document, the reader agrees that under no circumstances are is the author responsible for any losses, direct or indirect, which are incurred as a result of the use of information contained within this document, including, but not limited to, —errors, omissions, or inaccuracies.

Table of Contents

Introduction

I would like to thank you for purchasing the book, "Data Analytics: Insiders Guide to Master Data Analytics."

Analysis has become crucial in today's world. It is essential if you are thinking about starting a new business venture or even if you want to expand an already existing business. Think of a situation where you are working in a company and a particular department has decided to launch a new product onto the market. It is quintessential that analysis has been performed thoroughly to make sure that you have obtained all the information that you would require regarding the market conditions and various other factors that will help you in deciding the profitability and the potential success of the product launch.

However, not many people know what data analysis is. Data analytics might sound a little intimidating, but it is all about processing the huge volumes of data that a business collects over a period of time. Analyzing this data will help you in identifying trends that can be extremely helpful if you are

Introduction

planning on making any new changes to your operations or even if you are looking toward expanding your operations. In this case, data analytics will come in quite handy.

This book will help you in understanding what data analytics is all about, the different benefits it offers for the running of your business and the various techniques of data analytics used. It is quintessential to know about the various techniques that are made use of for analyzing the data because without this, all the data that you might have collected would be of little use. If you are well informed, you will be able to make the most suitable decisions that will help in the growth of your business.

Thank you for purchasing this book. I hope that you will be able to gather all the information that you had hoped to and that it will add to your business acumen.

Chapter 1:
The Basics of Analytics

This chapter will help you in understanding the basics of analytics. Analytics has been defined as the process of understanding the data by creating certain meaningful patterns. Analytics is a vital aspect in various types of businesses for understanding not just the performance of the business but also for quantifying such performance for better knowledge of trends. The most important aspect of analytics would be the visualization of data you already have on hand. Does this seem a little complicated to you? Why don't we take a look at an example so that you gain a better understanding of this?

For instance, as a homemaker, you are aware that there will be $10,000 coming into your home budget every month in the coming year. That's a lot of money, isn't it? Yes, it indeed is and being the responsible person that you are, you will perhaps want to keep a certain amount aside for the household expenditure. You will be able to keep an eye on all the expenses incurred and also analyze it. You can do this because you have had years of practice doing the same thing. This does make you quite powerful when it comes to analyzing. Data analytics is a powerful tool and, when made use of in a proper manner, it will help your business reach great heights.

Terms that you should know

What is cross-channel analytics? Does the thought of big data scare you and who would even know what "structured data" is? Unless you have previously been involved in data analytics or you learned a subject regarding the same in college, it is not likely that you are aware of these terms.

Analytics seem to be made up of certain complicated terms and phrases that can seem intimidating to anyone. Analytics can even intimate the most tech savvy webmasters and will want to make them dig deeper into the content that their website has been collecting over the last few years. You needn't worry about this, though. In this section, you will learn about the different basic terms that you should familiarize yourself with if you want to understand data analytics. This chapter should make your understanding of these terms easier.

Analytics

This is probably the most obvious term to start with. Analytics is the process of obtaining meaningful patterns from given data. When people talk about making use of analytics, it usually concerns a particular platform like Omniture or even Google Analytics, for instance, and this will help you in measuring the traffic that is coming through your website.

These platforms will also provide you information about not just where the traffic is coming in from and how much traffic is coming in. It also tells you the time that is spent by the visitors on particular pages. You can, therefore, start making use of analytics in a tactful manner. If you notice that the traffic to your website is high at a specific time, then maybe you can start making use of such information for publishing content that will tempt them to look further.

Behavioral Analytics

This method is about opting for an approach for analyzing and reading data that has a more human feel to it. It is also often referred to as a "holistic" approach. Don't let the name discourage you from reading more about it. Mostly, a behavioral approach for analytics will help you in building and gaining a better understanding of how and why online users tend to behave in the way that they do, by making use of data that doesn't always seem related.

Take, for instance, any social media interactions and also the sum of money that is spent on a particular site. The website from which the customer or the visitor navigated from and where they might next head toward. When looked at as one single experience, this will help you in understanding not just the intention of the visitor, but you will also be able to predict their future behavior. That gives you a real advantage.

Big Data

This is perhaps one of the most commonly used terms when it comes to data and it is crucial that you know the meaning of this term. Big data can be thought of as a convenient abbreviation for the massive amount of data that is available to you because of the online traffic that has, in turn, increased the need for having accurate analytics so that you can understand the data in a proper manner.

For instance, think about Amazon. This company would get massive amounts of data traffic. Not only will they have needed to have access to this data, but they would also have information about all the different customers who have visited their platform. This would include all the information about their orders, names, locations and even their browsing history.

Now, this indeed is "big data." Amazon has such a massive amount of data that it makes use of the third largest Linux databases in the world for helping it with its operations. Amazon doesn't only stop at collecting all this data. It makes use of this data for creating custom-made experiences for all the users who are registered on Amazon. This includes a personalized homepage and also a list of recommended products depending on their browser and order history. You may have noticed this as you browsed the website. All of this information helps to build business.

Bounce Rate

The rate of visitors who visit your site, and then leave it immediately after visiting just one page - instead of going through the other pages - is referred to as the bounce rate. A low bounce rate is good, and a high bounce rate means that your site has very little to interest the visitor. This is useful information because you need to keep the bounce rate manageable to ensure customers find sufficient information to keep them looking through your website.

Cross-channel Analytics

This is the ability to analyze data that is available from different channels like email, social media and mobile apps and so on. This data itself can be stored in different places and is used for getting a better understanding of the overall experience of the customer.

Data Cleansing

This is the process of detecting and, then getting rid of, certain inaccurate records that are present in your database. This data might be incomplete or even incorrect. This helps in getting rid of duplicate data as well. Mistakes can be caused due to various reasons and one of the most common mistakes is human error.

Data Quality

It is essential that the data that you are making use of is reliable. It needs to be accurate and accessible as well. If it weren't, then what good would it do?

Data Visualization

Data analytics isn't just about the text. Data visualization is also referred to as Dry Vis, and it will help in captivating the attention of the viewer. It is all about creating data analytics in a shareable way that is captivating and engaging.

Direct Traffic

This consists of the visitors who have accessed your site by typing in the URL of your website or they have clicked on the web address present in their bookmarks. Direct traffic will give you an estimate of the number of visitors who are already aware of your brand, and it shows consumer loyalty. This is very useful information as you can use this for loyalty rewards.

Machine Learning

This is a process that will allow a system to analyze the data and then learn about the action that it has to take instead of programming the computer to simply carry out one particular function. Machine learning is usually made use of for finding any patterns that aren't obvious to us. For instance, US retailer Target makes use of machine learning.

Target had decided to give discounts to couples that were expecting a child, a discount on all the items that they would require for dealing with parenthood. However, without this information, it would have been tough to figure all this out. Target hired a machine-learning expert and he helped in identifying the different buying habits of the individuals who had become pregnant. Once, they knew this, Target could devise a marketing campaign that targeted such people and offered them better deals on products related to pregnancy. This can apply to all kinds of users and give the company valuable data.

Search Data

This consists of all the data that you might have stored within your system that relates to the entire array of various search terms that people make use of in a search engine. These would lead them to click on your page from the results displayed. This information isn't easy to access though is exceptionally useful.

Search Traffic

This refers to the traffic that tends to visit a concerned website after they have clicked on the URL from the various results that are displayed by the search engine. This can include organic traffic as well as paid traffic. Organic traffic refers to the visitors who end up visiting or clicking on the unpaid or natural results that are displayed by the search engine. Paid traffic refers to those visitors who click on the listings. It makes a difference because your company needs to be high in the ranking to get great results.

Structured Data

Certain rules guide this data, and various programs, browsers and even search engines can easily read it. An example of structured data would be Schema markup. Structured data can reside within a file like a database or even a spreadsheet depending on the type of model that you are making use of and the various parameters like numeric, name, address and so on. You can also look up data depending upon different numbers and even characteristics like certain prefixes such as Mr., Ms., or Dr. Structured data can not only be stored and analyzed easily, but it is also easy to enter.

Unstructured Data

This seems like the rebellious sibling of the data that is mentioned above. Unstructured data, as the name suggests, has got no predefined model or any form of organization. It is tough to analyze and store. Searching for this data is not easy. One of the simplest examples of unstructured data would be the data that is present in an email.

You can sort your inbox using different filters like date, sender's name or even time. The one thing you can never sort it by is the exact content that is present in it. Multimedia is also responsible for the creation of unstructured data. One single document can contain an amalgamation of different forms of media like videos, images, audio and even slides. Not all this data can ever fit properly into an existing database.

Usually, businesses and various firms and companies tend to make use of analytics for understanding the workings of their operations. They tend to make use of the different analytical processes for the business data that they have gathered and then try to describe the same in quantifiable terms so that they can predict the performance of the company. They can also take the necessary steps for improving the performance of their business.

Over the course of this book, you will learn about all the different types of analytical techniques that businesses make use of for analyzing their data. Analytics makes use of various algorithms and functions that can seem quite complicated. Before moving onto the more complex topics discussed in this book, we should perhaps take a look at the various challenges and risks that you will most likely have to face if you start making use of analytics.

Challenges Posed

In the analytical industry, a lot of importance has been given to the ability to solve problems that the massive amounts of data would usually pose. Challenges are posed because the data or the information that has been obtained tends to keep changing frequently and continuously. This type of data is usually referred to as big data. Previously, this form of data used to be a problem for the scientific community alone. However, it tends to pose a threat to the entire business community as well, since most of the transactions are taking place online and involve huge amounts of data that are collected extremely quickly.

The next challenge that the analytics industry found it had to deal with is the actual analysis of the data that hasn't yet been structured. This form of data is referred to as unstructured data, and it differs from structured data mostly by the format that it subcultures. This kind of data can also never be stored in the various databases in which all sorts of data are usually stored. Unstructured data will simply have to be transformed into a form that can be stored in the database so that it can be usefully utilized. The content that we find in emails is a form of unstructured data. Such material tends to form the basis for business intelligence and it should, therefore, be stored in a proper manner for assessing the quality of the business and its performance as well.

For instance, if a firm can provide not only its employees but also the citizens of a particular country with doctor's notes so that they can claim insurance, then such an activity is considered to be fraud. The insurance companies can stop such a fraud if they start being vigilant about the way in which their data has been structured. In an estimate that was provided by McKinsey Global, after much research, it was noted that big data could be made use of for cutting down the spending of the American health care system and save more than $300 billion every year. That is a lot of money, isn't it? Imagine what this data could do for your company.

The different challenges that are present in the field of analytics have provided scope for a lot of innovation. This room for innovation has lead to the creation of various information systems that have in turn lead to the creation of various forms of machine analysis that will help in the better presentation of the big data. A notable innovation in this form of machine analysis is the introduction of a grid-like architecture that allows for multiple functions and processes to be performed simultaneously by equally distributing the workload to different computers that will help in the analysis of every unit of data that is present in the unit.

In recent times, analytics is also being made use of in the field of education. This is also true for different organizations within the government as well. It is a given fact that there exists a certain level of complexity within the analysis of the education sector. Educators have been trying hard not just to understand but also analyze the performance of every student by identifying certain patterns that exist in their performance.

It doesn't stop there. They have also been able to come to an approximation of the probability that the student has of succeeding or graduating. However, for doing this, they needed to first have knowledge themselves regarding the ways in which the data can be interpreted. If they were not able to interpret this data themselves, then it would be of no use. There are times when the data is too complex to be explained, or it is too difficult to grasp. For overcoming such a situation, there are a couple of analytical tools that have been developed for getting a better understanding of the data.

The other significant challenge that this particular industry has to face is the change that has come in the regulatory needs. There are certain industry-specific regulations, like in the banking sector. In this sector, all the banks will have to adhere to guidelines, rules and regulations like the BASE III. These guidelines are set in place for making sure that the banks don't become insolvent. There is also a need for the identification of the different models that will help them to assess risks. As you can see, the data is very specific to the needs of the company using it and a good understanding is required or how this information can help to better the performance.

Risks

Before explaining the different risks that the analytics industry has to face, let us look at an example. For instance, consider that there are only two products that are present in a given market. The two products are Product A and Product B. Product A cost $50 more than Product B. If both these products are providing the same benefits, then you would want to purchase product B. This condition would be referred to as price discrimination.

The same would apply to the analytics industry as well. If analytical software costs less than other alternatives, people might opt for the cheaper variety of analysis, and this could cause more issues. Most of the results that are produced by making use of analytical processes would have some level of variation. These results could, in turn, cause trouble with laws and rights that exist. Different complexities exist within analytics, but this isn't of much significance when it comes to the actual decision-making process.

Types of Analytics

Now that you are aware of what analytics is all about and you have also been given information about the different challenges and risks that the analytics industry has to face in today's market. In this section, let us take a look at the different types of analytics that are there. This will help you in getting a better idea of what analytics would be suitable for a particular situation. You might have understood by now that the main aim of making use of data analytics is for obtaining an insight into the trends that exist in the data that's been amassed so that you will be able to take better business decisions.

However, there are different types of analytics that you can make use of, and the results will vary depending upon the design of the analytical processes. It is really important that while building designs and for building a database - or even for starting to structure a business intelligence process - you will be able to provide an ecosystem that is versatile. You will be able to increase and optimize the input of data and you will also be able to analyze the diverse databases well. There are three types of analytics that you can make use of and, in this section, we will take a look at these three.

Predictive Analytics

This is the type of analytics that is usually made use of when it comes to forecasting. In this form of analytics, the data is converted into information that is precious, and it can also be used very easily. You can make use of this particular data and then determine the future outcome of a particular event. This will also help you in figuring out the probability of the occurrence of a future event. This particular type of analytics is made up of multiple techniques making use of statistics, and it is often made use of for machine learning or even data mining as well as game theory as well. You can make use of the various methods for analyzing the data that you have obtained in the present, and you can also make use of the data that already exists for analyzing future trends.

When you are viewing predictive analytics, solely from the perspective of business, then you will be able to notice that the models always concentrate on helping you capture the relationship that exists between various factors and the different specifications that tend to affect your data. You will be able to assess the different risk that is associated with all the factors mentioned above and apply it to your own specifications. You will also be able to get the hang of the different conditions that will help you in making a guided decision using that data. Three processes are usually included in predictive analytics and these are predictive modeling, decision analysis and its optimization, and the third one is transaction profiling.

Let us take a look at a few examples so that you will be able to understand the different ways in which you can make use of predictive analysis in your business. For instance, assume that your business tends to focus only on optimizing and then managing the relationship that your brand has with customers. Then you will be able to analyze all the data that you might have on customers and make use of the same for exposing any definite patterns that exist in the behavior of the various customers. Another example would be to consider a hypothetical situation where your business is offering multiple products to the customers. You will be able to get an idea of the behavioral patterns of the customers. This helps you predict the amount that your customers are willing to spend on the products made available by you.

This, in turn, will help you in understanding the spending habits of the customers. By understanding their spending habits, you will also be able to figure out the usefulness these products have for them. When you have all this valuable information available at hand, then you will be able to increase your profitability by providing for customer needs. Building stronger relationships with your customers also has the effect of being sure of the potential your company has in the given market. Every organization should make sure they invest some money in creating statistical algorithms. This can be created within the business or the organization, or by hiring of professionals who have a good record in this area as well. This team of data analysts will help in creating an algorithm for identifying the predictive patterns in the data that is already present.

Descriptive Analytics

Descriptive analytics can be thought of as a process that is usually made use of in data mining and even in business intelligence. In this method, you will be able to not only look at the data but also analyze all past events that are relevant. You will also be able to obtain an insight into the best methods that you can make use of for approaching any of the future events your company is planning. You can also make use of this process for analyzing and mining through all the data. By doing this, you can understand the reasons for failures in the past. This is an excellent method of analysis that will help you in understanding the various reasons for success as well as failure. You can also analyze the different relationships that are present in the data and be able to quantify these.

This is a great tool for analytics and it helps in classifying and grouping consumers. The descriptive models are extremely different from the previous model of analysis. They will help you in understanding the relationship that exists between the products or services offered by the company and the different consumers. You will be able to make use of this model for categorizing your customers based on the products they prefer and also assess their loyalty towards the company. This will also help you in developing different models for further analysis of large groups of data.

Prescriptive Analytics

This model of analytics will help you in optimizing and stimulating the data that you have for developing a model for the future. It helps in processing big data and also helps you in understanding the different rules of business for making accurate predictions regarding the company's future transactions. This process isn't simply about predicting future outcomes.

It will also provide you with helpful suggestions regarding the actions that you can take for the benefit of your company, from all the predictions that you have been able to make with the available data. You can understand the different implications of every single decision that you make. Not just this, but you can also predict the occurrence of an event, when it will occur and also the reasons for such a happening.

This model of data analytics will help you in understanding the different decisions that you can take and also the advantages of each important decision that you take. This is useful for any such event that might occur in the future, and also for the mitigation of risks. This will help you in understanding the implications of the decisions you take. Processing new data will also assist in improving any future predictions for making better decisions in the future. Prescriptive analysis can be thought of as a crossover between the different rules of business and the various mathematical models for analyzing data.

The input of data can be from both internal and external sources. You can obtain any data. It needn't be structured alone. Unstructured data, categorical data, numerical data and even ordinal data can be used. You will have to make use of different business policies to serve your understanding the different preferences, policies, practices and even different boundaries that you should set for the betterment of your business. By making use of applied statistics, you will be able to develop different mathematical models, and this will help you with machine learning.

When you start making use of this model of analytics, then you will be able to plan strategically. The health care industry needs this model for strategic planning by making use of data that is obtained from various external sources and factors like demographic trends, health needs and even the economic data. Planning for the future will also help you in getting to know whether or not you will be able to think about expansion.

Chapter 2:

Benefits of Big Data

B y now, you must be aware of the potential of the Big Data and data analysis, but aren't entirely sure of what good it could do for your business? Then this chapter will help you in making up your mind. Here are the practical benefits that you can reap through dependent data analytics and big data.

Creating a Dialogue with Consumers

Consumers in today's age are extremely tough nuts to crack. They don't easily make purchases and they like making informed decisions. Before making a purchase, they often like to look around for other options or browse through social media. They like being treated as unique, and then they expect to be thanked for making that purchase.

Big data will help you in profiling all such vocal and fickle consumers in a manner that can be thought of as a real-time conversation in this digital world. Don't think of this as a luxury. If they aren't treated the way they think they should be, then they will move to another source to make purchases without a second thought. For instance, when a customer enters a bank, then Big Data tools and platforms will allow the worker or clerk to check the customer's online profile and then learn about the relevant services or products that might interest the consumer.

Therefore, the consumer can also be made aware of the same when looking for a reliable purchase or service. Big data will also help you in uniting the two distinct spheres of shopping in both the digital sense and the physical one. For instance, a retailer can offer a discount on a mobile carrier, based on the need of a consumer that was expressed on social media.

Redeveloping your Products

Big data can also help you in understanding the manner in which others perceive your products. This will let you make any changes to your product line or marketing techniques to meet current trends. Analyzing unstructured data present on social media will allow you to understand the opinions of your customers and segregate them into different geographical locations or identify them from different demographic classifications.

Big data will also let you test different variations of several computer aided programs that will help you in checking and keeping track of all the minor changes like the effects of cost, lead times and also the performance of a product on the market. You can also adapt your production process according to the needs of the public.

Performing Risk Analysis

The success of your business depends on the way in which you handle your business dealings. However, there are several other social and economic factors that can affect your performance as well.

Predictive analytics that make use of big data will allow you to scan and then even analyze reports mentioned in newspapers and various other social media feeds. This will allow you to stay on top of the latest developments that are taking place in your respective field. This also allows you to perform various "health" tests that will help you in identifying if any of your customers or suppliers are at risk of defaulting any of their payments or orders.

Safekeeping of your Data

You will be able to take a look at the performance of your whole company by making use of the different analytical tools. This will allow you to identify if there are any internal threats. By mapping out the data landscape, you will be able to find if any sensitive information isn't protected in the manner in which it should have been. If it isn't, then you can make sure that you are storing it in an appropriate manner. With data analytics, if you notice that any credit card information hasn't been stored in a proper manner, then the same can be flagged to prevent any damage and also to avoid this happening in the future.

Creation of New Streams of Revenue

The various insights that you can gather from analyzing the market and its various consumers aren't just valuable to you alone. You can even sell them as trend data to any other bigger players in the market that are operating in the same segment.

This will help you in creating an entirely different stream of revenue for yourself. An impressive real life example would be the popular song identification application, Shazam. Shazam helps the record labels and music houses to identify where the different subcultures in music are coming from by monitoring the service it provides. This includes the tracking of the data regarding location that the mobile applications provide easily. This will enable the record labels to launch new artists who would suit the preferences of the audience or remarket the existing ones again. The criteria for using this app is that you want to know what a certain music track is and of course that means you, as a customer, are showing an interest in that music. That's useful information for record companies.

Customizing your Website

Big data will allow you to customize and personalize the content, feel and the look of your website. You can do so in real-time so that it can suit the needs of the different consumers who are entering it depending upon their sex, nationality or any other factor that leads them to your website. The best example of this would be the customized list of recommendations that Amazon provides. It does so by making use of a filtering technique that makes use of real-time data, and also the purchase history for suggesting other products. This is similar to the "People you may know" feature that is provided by LinkedIn and other various networking sites. This approach does work, and the data provided by Amazon shows that this has helped them in increasing their revenue by 20%.

Reducing the Cost of Maintenance

Usually, factories tend to have an estimate about the life span of a certain type of equipment and know how long it will last. As a result, they end up replacing such equipment within that assumed span of time, even if the machinery has got a few more years of useful life. Tools that analyze big data will be able to do away with such practices that aren't practical or even economical. These tools have got access to massive amounts of data and they can spot discrepancies quickly. They use this to estimate the average lifespan of the device. As a result, the business will be able to make use of a replacement strategy that has a greater utility and has less downtime. Faulty equipment can be tracked more easily.

Tailor-made Healthcare Plans

In the world that we are living in, personalization is the mantra. Healthcare is still one sector where the trend of personalization still hasn't caught up. When someone has been diagnosed with cancer, they will have to undergo therapy. If that proves to be ineffective, they will have to go to another doctor and so on. Wouldn't it be helpful if the cancer patient could receive medication that is tailor made to suit his genes? This will not only allow for the reduction of costs, but it will also help in achieving better results. Human genome mapping isn't a concept that's far away in the future, due to the leaps in medicine and technology. The kind of potential of big data in the healthcare system is vast.

Extensive Insights

If a business user wanted to analyze huge amounts of data, then it would be quite normal for the IT department to help them since they probably don't possess the technical skills for doing that. However, by the time they receive such information, it may have ceased to be of any use for them. Big data tools help in simplifying the work of the technical team by laying down the groundwork. Then they will simply have to develop algorithms that will help them in analyzing the data that is already available.

Every business tries to enhance the customer satisfaction that it can provide to improve their profitability. According to the needs of the company, the target markets of different businesses and industries as a whole keep on changing. The societal standards, needs and changing trends change the target audience as well. Being aware of this, it is quintessential to pull yourself ahead of all your completion through innovation and better services that will help in attracting and retaining customers.

Before business analytics has reached the stage it is at today, people in business had to make use of analytical models that were error-ridden. This potentially damaged their plans. Since it wasn't possible to extract and analyze data in a systematic manner, the earlier versions of analytics didn't prove to be of much use. The traditional teams that were involved in research and analytics had to spend long hours trying to gather information from all their customers. Statistical analysis helps in decision-making, and it requires the collection of data. Decision-making is a highly important process, and it shouldn't be overlooked at any cost. Even a minor error can damage the business. How exactly does analytics work and what are the benefits of making use of analytics in business? Let us take a look at the various advantages of making use of analytics in business.

Measuring Performance

Every business has a mission statement of its own. The mission statement represents the goals of the business and the value they are offering to their consumers. It could include their marketing plan or any other goal that they would want to achieve. Making use of the mission statement as a guideline, most businesses tend to either promote from within in an attempt retain their employees. This is a helpful manner in which the success of the company can be judged, but it wouldn't be prudent to leave the business depending on old established ideals.

Values must be capable of being quantified and they should be expressed in a tangible manner to generate profits for the business. Quantifying the values of the business will help in improving its analytical process since it will help in defining the goal of the business. When such values can be quantified, then the same can be conveyed to the employees to get a clearer view of what their performance should be like. The more informed the employees are, the better their productive will be. Fresh blood also helps with the generation of new ideas.

Better Decision-making

Being able to access important data will give your business the power to take better decisions. Not only will it provide you with viable information, but it will also help you in making effective and efficient decisions. Companies can also maximize the applicability of these analytics for sharing the same information with as many employees as possible. A group will be able to analyze the data better, and you will be able to make decisions that are more objective if the opinions of different people are being taken into account.

Provides Clearer Insights

The recent variations of analytics that have been developed give importance to the manner in which the data is being presented to the analytics team or department. Making use of detailed charts and graphs for better decision-making is a good idea. Visual representation not only makes it easier to grasp the gist of the analysis but also to understand it easily. With the visualization of data analytics, all the numbers and figures are simply presented in a concise manner through appealing and organized charts and graphs. This helps people who are not so technical to understand.

Stay Updated

Trends keep changing. With every new trend that comes into vogue, the consumers also tend to change their preferences. What might have been considered to be "in" a few months ago might be regarded as trashy now. Analytics will help you in gaining insights about the way in which your target audience thinks. It will help you in keeping in sync with all the various fads that keep coming and going. In this dynamic environment, if your business stays stagnant, there won't be any growth. If you want to protect your business operations from unpredictability, then make use of analytics for identifying the consumer trends and patterns that exist in the market. Keep innovating and improving by making use of the data obtained.

Provides Efficiency

It is quintessential that efficiency takes a top priority in operations for business. When you can gather large amounts of data, then you can make use of the same for improving your business efficiency. By analyzing this data, you will be able to make informed decisions that will help in making the most of any situation. Analytics will help in making the business more effective and efficient. Being aware of the needs of the dynamic market will help you in making better choices and also for determining the goals of the organization. You will also find that data will help you to overcome the seasonal lulls and cater for times when the company may be put under pressure.

Data analytics leads to something referred to as business intelligence. There are two meanings to business intelligence, which are closely related to the term intelligence. The first meaning is that you use the intelligence capacity of human beings and apply that to different activities and affairs of business. The intelligence of business is a relatively new field, which means being able to investigate the capability of the human mind to apply the cognitive faculties to manage and support the decisions made by businesses during any problematic situation or period.

The second meaning relates to the use of intelligence in the form of information, which is valued for its relevance and its currency. The intelligence is information that has been drawn from experts and the knowledge and technologies that are efficient at managing the organization and the working of the business. In this sense, business intelligence comprises a broad category of technologies and businesses that will help you gather and analyze the data, which will help you make better decisions about your business. You will be able to have knowledge of every factor, either internal or external, which will help you make a better decision for your business. It is always good for firms to have a great deal of knowledge about all the customers, business partners, economic environment, competitors and the internal operations to make excellent decisions for the business. You will be able to make these decisions when you use Business Intelligence.

There is a specialized area of business intelligence called competitive intelligence, which is based on understanding the competitive environment. You will be able to gather the information on how your competitors act and make decisions. You will also be able to make better decisions using this information. There is very little attention that is paid to gather internal information.

Most often in modern businesses, there are new standards, technologies and automation. These have led to the collection and the availability of vast amounts of data. There are data warehouse technologies that help in setting up repositories, which will help you store data. There are new tools that help you collect data with ease. Certain technologies have allowed the generation of reports to analyze data in a very fast way. Through business intelligence, you will be able to sift through huge amounts of data while helping you extract information that you need and also turn that information into knowledge upon which you can make the right decisions.

Chapter 3:
Techniques for Data
Analytics

Before getting started with the different techniques that are made use of for data analytics, let us take a quick recap about big data. Big data is the application of particular techniques and technologies for the processing of huge volumes of data. These sets of data are often quite complex and large so that use of on-hand management tools for databases has trouble in processing them. This includes data from web logs, any photographic archives, medical records and so on. Very large data means it requires a minimum storage space of one terabyte in a database. Did you know that Facebook makes use of 100 petabytes of storage for just pictures and videos?

In this chapter, we will take a look at the different data analytics techniques that can be made use of for analyzing big data. The methods that are widely used are of seven types, and they have been discussed in brief as follows:

Association Rule Learning

Is it likely that the people who purchase coffee are more or less likely to purchase carbonated drinks as well? This technique was first made use of by a major chain of supermarkets for discovering interesting relationships that existed between products and the consumers purchasing them by making use of data that was available to them from the point of sale system that is present in all supermarkets. This form of data analytics is usually used for placing products in a better location or changing their proximity for increasing their sales. These could be used for extracting information about the visitors to each website to increase the amount of sales, for analyzing any biological information that can help in uncovering newer relationships and for monitoring the system logs that will help in detecting if there were any malicious activities.

Decision Tree Analysis

How do you determine the category into which a particular document belongs? Classification of data, by making use of statistics, will help in identifying the different categories into which a particular observation belongs. For this method, there needs to be historical data; that is data from any past transactions. By making use of this statistical form of classification, you can group the existing data into different categories and also develop specific profiles of these categories. For instance, you can figure out the different profiles of students who enroll in online classes.

Genetic Algorithms

What TV programs should be broadcasted and at what time should they be telecasted for improving the ratings? Genetic algorithms, as the name suggests, have been inspired by the way in which evolution works. Evolution works through the various mechanisms of mutations, inheritance and importantly natural selection. These mechanisms can be made use of for evolving or making use of solutions for tackling problems and optimizing returns. For instance, they can be made use of for determining the schedule of the attending doctors in the ER in hospitals, for determining the various engineering practices and the various methods made use of for developing a fuel-efficient car. Or perhaps, they can be used for coming up with any business practice that can help capturing the attention of the target audience. All of this is essential to a business and the algorithms help the company to adjust its activities to go with the current trends.

Machine Learning

Which movie should a particular customer watch from a catalog consisting of hundreds of movies? What are the suggestions you should make to that customer? This can be decided by looking into the suggestions based on their viewing history. How does this even come into being? How does a machine know what to suggest? Machine Learning consists of making use of particular software that will help the machine to learn from the data it processes. It enables a computer to learn without having to specifically program it for the same and it focuses on the making of predictions by known properties that are fed into the system. Machine learning will help the computer in understanding the preferences of the user and provide a list of suggestions and give options regarding similar content and engage the customer. You may have noticed after having made a search for an item that you are presented with alternatives even when visiting a totally unrelated website. This is Machine Learning at its best. It learns about customer activity.

Regression Analysis

Does your age have any effect on the preference of a car that you might purchase? Regression analysis can be simply understood as the manipulation of an independent variable to see the influence it would have on a dependent variable. It helps in determining the way in which the dependent variable would change when the independent variable changes. This works best when it comes to unremitting quantitative data like speed or even age. Regression analysis is usually made use of for determining the level of consumer satisfaction and its impact on consumer loyalty, or perhaps the impact of the neighborhood on the listing price of a house.

Sentiment Analysis

How well is the new exchange policy of a particular business being received? Sentiment analysis helps in determining the emotions of the consumers on a given topic. It is usually made use of for improving the service that is provided by a hotel, or customizing any incentives that are being given to customers, or giving consideration to the opinions of the customers regarding a product from various social media sites.

Social Network Analysis

Social network analysis was made use of for the first time in the telecommunications field. Then it was adapted for usage in other fields as well. This is now made use of for analyzing the relationship between the people and the various commercial activities that they are concerned with. This helps in determining how an individual forms ties with different people, the individuals who are capable of influencing other people and is used for understanding the basic social structure that exists in any society. This helps in making use of social media for understanding the needs and requirements of a customer and providing them with the same.

In the following chapters, you will learn more about each of these different techniques. So, keep reading.

Chapter 4:
Association Rule Mining

A ssociation rule mining is the technique that is made use of for discovering or unearthing relationships that are hidden in the big data. Rules refer to a set or item sets that are identified, and these sets represent the hidden relationships within the data. The underlying objective of this method is the determination of the occurrence of one or more items that are present in the data set.

A machine doesn't supervise this method. There won't be any direct guidance regarding the output of data for finding any patterns in it. In most of the commercial environments today, huge amounts of data usually get accumulated within the databases on a daily basis from all the regular operations. This tends to lay down a foundation for the rules of the association. For instance, in a retail environment, the data relating to the purchases made by customers is collected on a daily basis at the checkout counters and even the online shopping transactions provide the same information when related to website purchases. This data that gets accumulated consists mostly of market basket transactions. Managers of various stores collect such data so that they can learn or identify any behavioral patterns regarding the purchases made by customers. This would enable numerous business related applications that are based on the different rules of data.

One famous example that depicts a strong association between the sales of two products would be the sale of diapers and the sale of beer. It was observed that most of the customers who tend to buy diapers also tend to buy beer. Investigation of transactions to establish this particular association might seem easy. However, we aren't talking about a couple of hundred of transactions, but it consisted of a few billions of transactions that take place across tens of thousands of different articles, and this has helped in identifying thousands of rules.

This helps in forming rules of associations by using algorithms. In retail markets, these rules help in identifying different and new opportunities for cross-selling certain combinations of products. For instance, Bread and milk would be a frequent item set and, in the same manner, examples of other market basket transactions could be bread, diaper, beer and eggs, milk, diapers, beer and cola, and bread, milk, diapers and beer. So, in this illustration, diapers and beer would be a frequent item set, and there exists a rule of association between diapers and beer. The idea of the association rule is based on the frequent item sets or market baskets that were formed. This is a simple illustration. However, it does ignore other essential market attributes such as the quantities of the items that were sold, the price of the items sold and also the brand of the items. The process of data mining would help in discovering hidden patterns in bigger transactions. One of the major challenges that this method would have to overcome would be the sheer number of the transactions within a data set. In other words, there's a need to develop a strategy that will help in working on big datasets so that frequent item sets can be identified. Sub-sampling of the dataset might lead to an increase in the chances of the discovery of certain frequent item sets and patterns.

Another challenge that one will have to overcome while performing the association rule analysis would be the uncovering of certain patterns that aren't true and are just a case of sheer dumb luck and nothing else. Therefore, there needs to be a lot of fine tuning done to an application before it can be made use of properly or become foolproof. The undiscovered patterns should be useful. To provide a clear set of rules, the product portfolio, customer relations and various other configuration options should be cleared up.

The applications of association rules help in understanding the purchase patterns and behavior of the customer to enable different applications of the same data. These rules will help in discovering new opportunities and different ways in which cross selling of products can be performed. It helps in coming up with personalized promotional and advertising campaigns, better management of inventory, clearer product placement strategies and an overall improvement in the customer relationship policies. There are various algorithms that are usually made use of for identifying the "frequent item sets" to arrive at association rule learning. The most frequently used and the most popular algorithm that is made use of is the Apriori algorithm. Different algorithms pose different advantages and disadvantages. Therefore, an algorithm has to be opted for while keeping in mind the required result.

There are various machine-learning algorithms that are usually made use of for data mining and for working with data in the numeric format. Some algorithms can be quite mathematical. However, association rule of data analytics doesn't involve anything more than regular counting and is best suited for categorical data. Association rule learning is all about finding certain connections that tend to occur in a collection of items. This is also referred to as Market Basket Analysis. The original application of this analysis was association mining.

The essential goal was to find certain associations of items that work well together and were, more often than not, purchased together. As mentioned earlier, the famous example would be that of diapers and beer. The simple explanation is that the men who go to a store to buy diapers, end up purchasing beer as well. This can be illustrated with the help of a few simple transactions showing the retail transactions of a particular store. For instance, let us suppose that a store has had 600,000 transactions altogether. About 7500 transactions were made for diapers, 60000 for beer and 6000 transactions were made for both beer and diapers together. If there didn't exist an association between beer and diapers, or they were both found to be independent of each other, then the only explanation would be that 10% of all diaper purchasers would also purchase beer. However, it was discovered that about 80% of the purchasers who purchased diapers also ended up purchasing beer. This is an increase of over 8 times what was to be expected. This is referred to as a Lift, the ratio of frequency for the occurrence of the same combination.

This can be determined with the help of simple counting of the various transactions present within the database. In the present case, the rule of association would state that the purchasers of diapers are likely to purchase beer as well with a Lift of 8. Statistically speaking, Lift is nothing but the ratio of the joint probability of two variables divided by the individual probabilities of the specific items. It can be stated as follows:

Lift = P (x, y)/ P (x) P (y). P (x) is the probability of one item, and p (y) is the probability of the other one.

The above illustration is fictional, and it is extremely rare for a case to have a Lift factor that is as high as 8. However, there is one case that occurred at Walmart, where it did happen. When a series of hurricanes struck Florida, Walmart mined their database to see what the customers had wanted to buy before the onset of the hurricane. They discovered that there was one particular item whose sales had increased by a Lift of 7. You might think that this item would be something that is essential for survival like batteries, bottled water, canned food, flashlights or something else related to survival. Well, it wasn't something like this at all. The one item was strawberry flavored pot tarts! Can you imagine a situation where people are queuing up to buy something as trivial as pop tarts? In spite of the obvious reasons - like the ease of storage, the fact that they don't have to be refrigerated or heated, that they are a good breakfast option and so on - it still came as quite a surprise to the analytical team at Walmart. So, Walmart took this as their cue and stocked up on Strawberry pop tarts before the next hurricane, and they managed to sell every single unit of this product.

Another example of association rule of analytics is quite fascinating. A professor at George Mason University taught about earth sciences and various systems of geoinformation.

He made use of this particular algorithm for determining the basic characteristics of a hurricane like the wind speed, atmospheric pressure, rainfall, direction, and so on. He discovered that there is an association that lies between the final strength of the hurricane and the values of all the different characteristics. He could predict the increase in the intensity of the hurricane and also the final strength of the hurricane better than by making use of the standardized model that's usually used. This algorithm, which was developed for business use, can also be used to track other geological and scientific events.

Let us take a look at one last illustration so that you get a better understanding of this concept. A major electronics store sold video cameras and VHS (video players or recorders). They went through their records of the customer database and they soon discovered that the customers who happened to buy a VHS used to come back after a period of about three to four months to purchase a video camera also referred to as a camcorder. The store made use of this particular information, and it designed a tailor-made marketing strategy by sending out discount coupons to the existing buyers who had purchased a VHS to give them the incentive to purchase a camcorder. Apparently, this did the trick. The success they enjoyed was due to association rule analytics. With the huge amount of data that is available and the powerful technology at our disposal, we can make use of this for developing better marketing strategies that will help in improving the profitability of the business. Who knew counting could help in such a drastic fashion?

Chapter 5:
Decision Tree Analysis

A decision tree is perhaps the most systematic of all the decision-making tools. These come in handy while dealing with a situation that has multiple stages and is quite complex. For instance, you need to plan and organize a sequence of decisions and also take into account the different choices that you have had to make at an earlier stage. The outcome of the probable external events will help in determining the types of decisions that you might have to take at a later stage in this sequence. A decision-making tree can be thought of as a diagrammatic representation of the different decisions, the external factors and events that bring in uncertainty and the various outcomes of all the probable decisions as well as events, in an organized manner. Let us take a look at an example to help you to get a better understanding of the decision tree.

In this example, suppose that your parents might visit you over the weekend. The two probabilities are that they might or might not come. If they do visit you, then you can go to the movies along with them. If they don't visit you then, depending upon certain external factors, you can make different plans for yourself. If the weather is favorable, then you can decide to either go for a swim or play your favorite sport. If the weather is unfavorable, then you can stay inside and watch movies. If the weather is favorable and you are running short of funds, then you can perhaps go to the movies and, if you have sufficient funds, then you can go shopping.

There are multiple possibilities and every possibility has got different outcomes. This was a simple illustration. Now think about the most complicated data regarding decision-making. For making things easier, it would be simpler if you start mapping the various situations, the probable outcomes for each situation and the different factors that need to be taken into consideration while thinking about the likely outcomes in each situation.

Each path that you draw in a decision tree will lead to a particular outcome. The result would vary depending upon the different courses of action that you opt for. You can also represent each of these steps in monetary terms, and this will help in making the process of decision-making much simpler. The result is quite simple. You simply need to decide about the most suitable course of action that you can take. You can weigh the benefits of each step against the different factors that you will have to take into consideration. If you think that more than one option seems to be beneficial then, in such a case, you should recalculate all the costs and risks involved in quantifiable terms so that you can opt for the route that is the most profitable of the lot.

Tips for Creating a Decision Tree

Here are some tips that you can make use of while making a decision tree.

- While starting the tree, always start with a rectangle towards the left edge of the page and proceed from left to right. This rectangle would depict the first node and, in here, you should write down the main issue or the first question that you have to ask.

- Start adding branches for every possible alternative that you can think of and start out by drawing separate lines to lead you to every likely outcome or solution that is a potential. These branches should start moving away from the primary node, towards the right side of the page. In the above illustration, your branches could be whether or not your parents would come and visit you.

- Once you are done adding branches, proceed towards adding leaves to this tree. Each leaf should be attached to the branch. These leaves can have another question or a condition that is attached to that particular solution.

- You can keep adding branches if you think you can arrive at different outcomes from the nodes of the leaves. You will need to label each branch once again as you have done in the previous step.

- Keep on adding leaves and branches till you feel that you have managed to include every single question and condition that is applicable. You should be able to reach a logical outcome by the end of this mind mapping. Terminate the branches once you think all your questions have been sufficiently answered. Once you are done with drawing the tree, you should verify the accuracy of all the points that you have noted down.

Advantages of Using a Decision Tree

Various advantages are available to you and you will benefit from this form of classification.

Decision trees will help you in performing the function of screening of different variables as well as a selection of features. Feature selection or the testing of variables is a critical role in decision-making. When you start making a decision tree, the first few branches or the nodes are the most important variables that have to be taken into consideration. This would automatically help you in figuring out the important factors of decision-making.

When it comes to data trees, the effort that goes into the preparation of the presentation of data is comparatively less. For instance, if you are making use of a dataset that comprises of variables running into millions, then you will need to scale it down before you can make use of any form of regression analysis on it. You needn't bother with such conversions in this method. The structure would essentially remain the same regardless of such a conversion. Another feature is that this method will also help you in saving the time wasted prepping the necessary data. Missing values wouldn't pose any problem since this wouldn't result in any structural discrepancy. Decision trees are not only easy to make but easy to understand as well.

Any non-linear relationships that might exist between different parameters wouldn't have any effect on this particular method. For instance, a simple regression analysis would fail if there were nonlinear relationships that exist between the variables that are being taken into consideration in this particular regard. Decision trees have got no use of any assumptions regarding any form of linearity that might exist in data. We can also make use of this in different scenarios where you know that the parameters aren't related linearly.

Chapter 5: Decision Tree Analysis

The most obvious advantage of this form of data analytics is the ease of interpretation. It is critical to explain a decision tree. These benefits make this an excellent option for the analysis of data. There is one thing that you should keep in mind while working with this model. Don't limit the growth of the tree and make sure that you include all the different aspects of the given data.

Chapter 6:
Genetic Algorithms

I n this chapter, you will learn about genetic algorithms, but before getting started, let us take a look at some algorithms for analytics that will enhance the results you obtain. These algorithms make your life easier by helping you obtain the results in the simplest form with you either having to do minimal or absolutely no work at all!

What does it do?

This algorithm makes use of data that has been classified. The algorithm works towards forming a new way of sorting the data using a decision tree. It is for this simple reason that the data must be classified beforehand.

The C4.5 creates a classifier when it is looking for a way to organize the data into a decision tree. So what is this classifier? It is a tool that works towards analyzing a particular group or category that the new set of data constitutes.

Chapter 6: Genetic Algorithms

Let us take an example of a set of students in a classroom. You know the way each student performs, and you have also gathered a fair idea about the habits of the students along with their strengths and weaknesses. This information is referred to as the attribute of the student. Now, you want to use all these attributes to gather information on the number of students who will successfully graduate this year. This algorithm uses the data that it has on each student and creates a decision tree, which will help you obtain the final decision. However, what are decision trees?

Well, a decision tree is a flowchart that will help you classify new data. The advantage of a decision tree is that you can create different events that may occur to the same person. Let us use the same example as above. The student has always graduated, the student has a high chance of graduating, the student is extremely distracted, or student will not graduate.

At each of the points that have been mentioned above, the algorithm will try to allocate a value to the student and will offer you this with the decision tree thereby giving you the answer you need.

You may now ask me why it is that you should use this software when you can make the decision tree on your own. Well, the fact is that there is a chance that you will make a slight error. With the algorithm, there is no possibility of an error, and you will be able to read the final data with no difficulty.

K – Means

The algorithm mentioned above uses the process of identifying a classifier. This algorithm uses clustering as the central idea.

This is a highly popular technique of cluster analysis that helps in the exploration of a dataset. This algorithm creates groups of clusters in which all the members within the cluster are similar in some way.

A genetic algorithm is a method of data analysis that makes use of artificial intelligence as well as computing. This is usually made use of for optimizing the solutions for any issues by making use of the theory of natural selection and evolution. Genetic algorithms are an excellent method in which you can sift through the extremely complex amount of data and huge volumes of data as well. These are considered to be capable of coming up with a reasonable solution for a complex issue. This was the generic meaning of a genetic algorithm.

Let us take a look at the technical definition of "genetic algorithm" that is available. A genetic algorithm takes inspiration from evolution and makes use of concepts such as selection, mutation, recombination and even inheritance for solving an issue. The most commonly employed method of genetic mutation would be the creation of a group of individuals who have been indiscriminately picked up from a given group. These individuals would then be evaluated by making use of an evaluation function that is given by the programmer.

Individuals would then be given a score that will highlight their fitness in any given situation. The two best people are picked up from this information and are then used to create one or more progeny after which certain random mutations are done on such an offspring. According to the needs of the application, this procedure will keep on going until you have arrived at a solution that is acceptable or you have gone through a particular number of generations. A genetic algorithm differs from the classical algorithm in two basic ways. A classical algorithm generates a single point at every iteration, whereas a genetic algorithm generates a population of points at every iteration. The second difference lies in the manner in which genetic algorithm helps in the selection of the subsequent population. That is done through a computation that is made up of a certain number of random generators. On the other hand, a traditional algorithm merely chooses the next point through deterministic calculations.

When compared to the tradition AI, a genetic algorithm offers more advantages. It is considered to be more robust and less susceptible to breakdowns due to any variations in the inputs.

Genetic algorithms are usually made use of in different fields like robotics, automotive designs, telecommunications and molecular design and so on.

Genetic algorithms are considered to be an excellent way in which you can solve a problem for which policyholders is known. They are very generic and can therefore work in any search space. All that you have to do is come up with an answer that will allow you to do well and a genetic algorithm will help you in creating a solution that is of high quality. Genetic algorithms make use of the principles of natural selection as well as evolution while solving any problem.

These algorithms are designed to do well in a particular environment where there is a large set of feasible solutions and in a search space that is extremely uneven. Genetic algorithms are well suited for any given environment, but these aren't always the best choice. Algorithms that are more specific to a situation and work in a much simpler space can easily outmatch them. They can also take up a lot of time to run and aren't always feasible to run in real time.

However, you will be able to create high-quality solutions in a given scenario. Let us take a look at a few keywords so that this chapter would make more sense. An individual refers to a probable solution; a population is a group of such individuals or people. Search space consists of all the probable solutions.

Chromosome refers to the blueprint of any given individual, traits are the aspects regarding an individual, an allele is the probable settings for a particular trait, a locus is the position of a gene in the chromosomes and a genome is the collection of all the chromosomes of a particular individual.

Basis in Science

During the mid-1800s, a British naturalist by the name of Charles Darwin published a book that changed the way in which human beings had been viewing this world. In his book entitled "The Origin of the Species," Darwin suggested that God didn't put human beings and all the other creatures on the Earth. However, they have evolved from other creatures and aren't unchanging.

At that time, the idea sounded preposterous and even blasphemous to a certain degree. Evidence keeps coming up, again and again, to prove that he might have been correct. The various advancements in our technology have given us the ability to read our DNA as well as that of the other creatures. Doing this has allowed us to understand that our DNA isn't much different from that of other creatures.

One brilliant example of this would be the Galapagos Islands, which are located in the Pacific Ocean, off the coast of Ecuador. These islands hold some striking instances of evolution as well as adaptation. These islands contain species that aren't found elsewhere. Several species of birds found on this planet share several characteristics that are too similar for it to be a coincidence.

There is a theory that suggests that these birds were blown to this island by winds and they were unable to get back to where they came from. So, over a period of time, these birds spread through the islands and began to adapt themselves to their new environment to survive. Several birds developed strong beaks for cracking hard nuts, narrow ones for pecking at insects and so on. These birds that were blown to the island had developed certain characteristics that helped in their survival, and this gave them a better chance at reproduction.

Therefore, this allowed their offspring to inherit some of their unique characteristics. Those without these characteristics simply perished after a while and eventually all the birds present on this island had a particular type of beak that would help in their survival. This is the process of natural selection and evolution. The individuals don't change. Instead, the ones that have survived will have a better chance at being fitter or surviving for longer. This keeps on happening, and it will lead to the production of offspring who have got a better chance at survival. It was only the process of continuous development and improvement that helped in the creation of genetic algorithms.

Chapter 6: Genetic Algorithms

Basics of Genetic Algorithms

The most common form of a genetic algorithm works as follows. A population is created with the help of a group of individuals who are chosen at random. The people in this community are evaluated. A programmer gives the function of evaluation, and this gives each of these individuals a specific score regarding how well they have performed in a given task. Two individuals are then picked from this lot based on their fitness and their naturally high chance of being selected. These individuals will then reproduce to generate one or more offspring. These offspring are mutated in a random manner. This keeps on going until a suitable solution has been obtained, or a sufficient number of generations have passed according to the programmer.

Selection

While there are different ways in which selection can take place, the most common type is the roulette wheel method. In this method, individuals are given a probability of their selection that is directly proportional to their scores of fitness. Two individuals would be selected at random and then they produce an offspring. You can make a simple algorithm on your own and that is the only way in which you will learn how to compile.

Now that you have selected two individuals are random, you know that you should get started with the production of an offspring between these two people. How do you go about doing this? The common solution is referred to as a crossover. The most commonly used form is that of a single point crossover. In a single point crossover, you can select one locus and then swap this with the remaining alleles from one of the parents with the other. An offspring would derive one section of the chromosome from one parent. The point at which the chromosome has been broken down usually depends on a point that has been randomly selected. It is referred to as a single crossover since only one point of crossover is present. Sometimes only one or more progeny are created, and then they are put into the new population. There is no crossover here. At times, it also happens that there is no crossover, and the parents themselves are directly copied into a new population.

Mutation

After the selection and crossover are done, you will have a whole new set of individuals or population present. Some of these would be direct copies, and others would be the result of crossover. To make sure that not all these individuals are the same, there needs to be a small scope for mutation as well. When you are looping these alleles, if that particular allele is selected for mutation, then you can change it by a small fraction or change it completely if you want to. Mutation is quite simple and it is all about changing the alleles that are selected.

Applications

Genetic algorithms are an efficient manner of finding a reasonable solution for a complex issue. Though the results aren't immediate, they do help in sifting through large volumes of complicated data. These can be effectively made use of in a search space without much information. You can also make use of this when you know what the solution is supposed to be, but you aren't aware of the manner in which you should do it. This technique helps in solving problems in ways you never thought of. On the flipside, they can give you certain answers that might be suitable for a test environment and not for real time usage.

Now that you are aware of what genetic algorithms are all about, you should get started with coding. You will be able to get the hang of it only through coding. Over a period of time, with practice, it will get easier.

Chapter 7:
Machine Learning

Traditional tools of data analytics aren't always the best-suited tools for capturing the essence of big data. The sheer value of this data is too big for a comprehensive analysis and the range of varied data that exists in the form of correlations between two sources of data that aren't similar. Traditional tools for data analytics aren't cut out for grasping the complete value of big data.

An analyst wouldn't be able to test all the hypotheses that exist and determine the true value that is hidden in all this data. The basic tools for analytics that are usually made use of in a business or in an enterprise for reporting help in reducing the reporting sums, various counts, running simple averages, as well as SQL queries. Online processing can be thought of as the systematized extension of all the basic analytics that are still dependent on a human being for directing them towards the specified activities for which calculations should be done. Machine learning is a really good option for making the most of the different opportunities that are hidden within the big data.

It helps in obtaining value from big and dissimilar sources of data with as little reliance placed on human direction as possible. Programming drives it, and it runs at a machine scale. This method is well suited while dealing with extremely complex data variables and where huge amounts of data are involved.

Unlike all the traditional sources of analysis that exist, this particular type tends to thrive on the increasing number of datasets that are involved. The greater the amount of data that is being fed into the system, the more it will be able to learn and then apply the same for the purpose of gaining better insights. When it is free of any constraints that might be placed on it due to the thinking capacity of the human mind, machine learning will help you in discovering and displaying the different patterns that are buried within the data.

Recently, many companies have been focusing on the ways in which they are storing data and also the management of the same. How can you make the most of the big data that you have and what is the best way in which you can process this? Should you save it on the premises or store it on a cloud? These are obvious questions, but then they don't provide you with the reason why big data is such a big deal. Only by making use of advanced analytics will a company or business be able to make the most of the data that it has on hand. The best way in which newer insights can be obtained would be through machine learning. This advanced technology of analytics that we make use of will help your business in generating reports regarding future scope and performance based on the past reports and other trends that are hidden in the data. The value of machine learning lies in the ability of the program to develop models that will generate accurate results and will also help you in guiding your future actions by discovering certain patterns that are present in the data that have never been noticed before.

There seems to be a lot of confusion regarding what machine learning is all about. Most of the software vendors claim that it helps in performing predictive analysis, deep learning, as well as machine learning. It is important that you understand what each of these things means so that you will know what you can expect from your vendor or buyer for each of these items.

Machine learning can be simply thought of as the modern science that has the potential to help you in finding any patterns as well as making certain predictions that exist in the data based on data mining, recognition of patterns and predictive analytics and related techniques.

Machine learning methods are best suited for situations that require insights that are deep and predictive and the same needs to be uncovered from sets of data that are so voluminous that traditional methods cannot be used. Machine learning is a better option than the traditional methods because it provides accuracy, speed and even scale while going through big data. For instance, it can detect fraud in a fraction of a minute. While doing so, machine learning takes into account the information associated with such transactions, the location and value. It also makes use of any historical data or data available on social networking sites for preventing any potential fraud.

Machine learning methods are more sophisticated when it comes to identifying the potential customers that exist and for churning out information about potential customers from different sources like social media and other CRM sources. Machine learning will assist in the analysis of the entire big data instead of just a sample. This not only allows for a predictive analysis that rests on sophisticated algorithms, but the results generated are accurate as well. For all those who are trying to make use of and who are also developing machine learning, it is not just important to provide accurate and predictive insights. It needs to be quick as well. Apart from these basic requirements, the data should be delivered in a meaningful manner, the operations should take place in a smarter manner and the results should be produced in usable forms.

While comparing the software for the analytics of big data, there are certain things that you should keep in your mind. These things are mentioned as follows:

You will need software for machine learning that is best in its class. Due to the sheer size of the data that is involved and the variety of the data, most of the traditional techniques will not be of much use. Analytical solutions that make use of machine learning are the most well suited options for analyzing dynamic data and even large amounts of unstructured data. The machine learning should be suitable for your business concerns.

A typical organization will make use of a machine learning software that will help in developing models that help in predictive analysis and help in churning out data that will curb frauds and generate patterns that are of some commercial use. Therefore, it is really important that the machine learning software that you have opted for can be easily integrated into the software environment in the enterprise. In this extremely competitive world, you will need an interface that will help in giving quick and effective solutions. As a result of this precondition, you will need an analytical platform that will help you in not only obtaining fast results, but it should also be easy to use, even if the group of users is quite diversified.

In the world of big data that we live in, there has been a paradigm shift towards making use of machines for the process of decision-making. There is great potential within big data, and we have all got the opportunities for making the most of these. Harvest all the possible patterns that you can make out of the data and then apply the same to your business for its development. Do you simply want to store or hold onto data? Or do you want to put it to some good use that will prove to be profitable for you?

Chapter 8:
Regression Analysis

Regression analysis is a statistical tool that is made use of for understanding and also for quantifying the relationship that exists between at least two more variables. Regressions could be something simple to extremely complex equations. There are two basic functions of making use of regressions in business and these are for forecasting as well as optimization of operations. Not just this, but it will also assist the managers in predicting future demand for the products or services. It can also help in fine-tuning the manufacturing as well as delivery processes.

In the most basic form, regression analysis can be thought of as the ratio that exists between any two given variables. For instance, you may want to evaluate the growth of meat sales (MS growth) based on the economic growth (GDP growth). The past data shows that one and a half times the economic growth represents the development in meat sales. Then the regression equation for the given situation would be: MS growth= GDP growth *1.5. The relationship between any two variables usually involves a constant. If the meat sales are increasing, and are growing at 1 percent in a stagnant economy, then the equation would be as follows: MS growth= (GDP growth*1.5) +1.

The variables that you are trying to make use of for an estimate are referred to as dependent, and the variable that you are making use of for predicting this dependent variable is referred to as independent. Regression can have one single dependent. However, the number of independent variables that can be present is unlimited, and these is usually referred to as "multiple regressions" if it makes use of more than one independent variable. Models of regression can also be made use of for pinpointing relationships between variables that are more complex. At times, a model might also make use of a square root or any other power or one or more of the independent variables mentioned for determining the dependent one. This would make the regression a non-linear one.

The most popular use of regression analysis in business is for predicting the events that are yet to happen. Demand analysis, for instance, will help you in predicting the number of units that the consumer might purchase. There are several other key factors that influence demand and these are dependent on various models of regression. Predicting the number of potential shoppers who would pass through a given billboard or the number of viewers of the Super Bowl will provide the management with essential information that will help them in managing their advertisement strategies. Insurance companies usually make use of regression analysis for finding out an approximate estimate of the number of policy holders who might be involved in accidents and so on for getting an estimate of the number of claims that would be made.

Another important use of a model of regression would be for the optimization of a process of business. A factory manager might be interested in finding the relationship between the temperature of the oven and the shelf life of the goodies baked. A call center might want to know the relationship that exists between the wait time and the number of complaints that they have received. This will help in improving productivity in business and it is a statistical tool that is frequently made use of by businesses in manufacturing and service sectors alike. As mentioned earlier, regression analysis helps in establishing the relationship that exists between two variables. The aim of the investigator would be to ascertain the effect one variable would have upon the other. For instance, the effect an increase or decrease in price would have upon the demand for a certain commodity.

Regression analysis is made use of for estimating the strengths and the direction in which the variables are related. For instance, if x and y are linearly related, then x would be referred to as independent variable and y would be referred to as dependent variable. Regression analysis can be of two types as mentioned earlier. Depending upon the number of independent variables, it would be given its classification. If there is one independent variable, then it is referred to as simple regression, and if there is more than one, it is known as multiple regression analysis.

Regression analysis can be made use of for computing several assumptions for the working of the business. There are several critical tests that you can make use of for ensuring that you get the right results from the various assumptions that you have made. These tests will ensure the accuracy of the regression analysis. There are various reasons for which regression analysis can be used. It can be made use of for determining the impact that would be there on the profits of a corporation due to an increase in price. It helps in understanding the relationship between the sales of a corporation and the changes in the advertising expenditures. It also helps in figuring out the ways in which stock price would be affected due to a change in the rates of interest. Regression analysis is usually made for predicting any future demands. There are specialized calculators and spreadsheet programs that are specifically made use of during a regression analysis due to the complexities involved.

Chapter 9:
Sentiment Analysis

How many emails do you receive on a daily basis? How many times does your phone ring on a daily basis? What about the messages on various social media platforms and on digital feedback forms? The amount of inflow of communications is quite high. There will be multiple teams constantly working to make sure that your business seems responsive. The customers who write emails or forward any form of communication from their end will expect a response from your end. However, it isn't just about being responsive. In your rush to get a response out, you might fail to see the bigger picture. The key to your success is all the inbound communications that you have been receiving.

Until now, mining of opinions has never been a major concern for companies. After all, isn't it enough work having to manage and maintain the information provided to the customers and the related data? Now you have got to worry about the sentiments that underlie such data? It might seem tedious, but it isn't. In fact, this is a really good way in which you will be able to improve the perception of your brand or business by the public. The underlying sentiment will help you understand the public perception of your business. Buried within all the text that you keep receiving, there will be information about the true standing of your business. You might be making use of your inbound data for keeping track of the details like the sales and information about the customers, but if you aren't able to see the underlying emotions that have been portrayed in these messages, then you should look again. This is where you will need to make use of sentiment analysis.

For so many years, businesses have been focusing on investing serious money into various data management tools. The cash that they have been pumping into the different platforms and various other software services has been with the sole aim of handling their data in a fashion that is more effective. These efforts are perfectly understandable. In the last two years, more data has been created than in the entire history of the human race up until now. The volume of data seems to be exploding. However, for all these investments made, sentiment analysis is a tool that still stays humbly in the background. For the different advantages that it offers, it is underrated. Businesses keep logging in millions of interactions, but no one is capable of listening to all of these interactions.

So, what exactly is sentiment analysis all about and why is it such a big deal? To put it simply, sentiment analysis software will help in extracting the meaning from within the millions of online communication that a business receives on a daily basis.

It helps in analyzing the stream of incoming messages and gauges the negative or the positive feedback that your business is receiving. This is used to gain an overall feel of the public opinion about your business. Text analytics drives data intelligence. The algorithm that is contained in this software will help in training and identify the difference between the various feelings that are hidden in the content. This software will help in analyzing the syntax used and the underlying tone of the content. This will help in understanding the true feelings of the customer towards your business.

Now, you will not only be better equipped with the necessary knowledge for understanding the attitude and the trends of your own business. You will also be able to improve the overall public sentiment towards your business by seeming to be more proactive. When you start thinking about the various retailers who make use of big data, you will notice that they have a fair margin for sentiment analysis. This is one new trend in data analytics that is here to stay.

This indeed is a recent addition to the industry. However, it shouldn't be perceived as a luxury. Businesses have managed to survive without all this until now, have they not? However, does this mean that they shouldn't pay heed to this fairly new entrant? Well, the answer would have been yes if customer experience didn't count. In the recent past, companies and businesses had been fighting it out to provide the best experience to the customers as was possible.

Customer experience is an incredibly important part of being able to conduct business successfully. When a customer is happy with the service that he or she receives, then it is very likely that the same customer will come back to you again. However, if they don't have a good experience, then that would probably be the last you see of them. It doesn't stop there. With the ease of access to the social media sites that exist these days, one word of bad publicity about your business can cause some serious damage.

There's another undeniable truth. Customers today have got access to pretty much anything they want from anywhere in the world. They can find the item that they like for the price that they are willing to pay. If you want to stay on top of the game, then you will need to take this seriously. By providing an exceptional service, you will be able to make the cut. Sentiment analysis helps in doing just this.

Emotions do translate into money these days. Do you remember the when Coca-Cola had come up with its "Share a Coke" campaign? It managed to take the world by storm and the declining trend in the soft-drinks market was turned upwards. How about the "real beauty" campaign that was started by Dove? These campaigns went viral and they were viewed and shared a couple of million times over various social networking platforms. The one thing these advertisements have in common is that they appealed to the public on an emotional level. Tapping into the emotions means you have gained their loyalty. Sentiments are extremely important. Play them well, and you have got a loyal customer base. The opposite of this might not be good news for your business. Therefore, don't think about writing off about the sentiment of public and make the most of it instead.

Creating a Model of Sentiment Analysis

This document will help you in analyzing a text string or an email and classify it with one of the labels that have been provided for determining whether it is positive or negative, happy or sad/ frustrated.

The first step would be the collection of all the necessary data. You will have to train your sentiment model against certain types of data that you would notice while making use of your model. For instance, if you are trying to determine the sentiment of all the tweets, then you should perhaps obtain the examples of the tweets you are targeting. Look out for texts like "feeling blue," "OMG, it is such a beautiful day" and so on. If you want your model to be any good, then you will need to feed in several hundreds of examples at least. All the text will have to be in the same language.

The second step is regarding labeling the data. Once you have got all the training samples, then you will need to classify all these samples according to certain labels. A label is something that would help in describing a certain text string. For instance, if the text string was "Feeling kind of blue" then you can label it as sad. If the text string was "OMG, it is such a beautiful day" you can label as "excited." You can create as many labels as you feel you need. However, make sure that there are at least a few dozen examples for describing each one of these labels. Labels can also be case sensitive. If you write the same word in lower case and then again in upper case, then the system will think that these are two different labels. For avoiding any mix-ups, it is advisable that you practice using only lower case. Only one label can be assigned to every line, and you cannot have multiple labels for the same text.

The next step is the preparation of the data. You can make use of Google Prediction API for training the data that is formatted as a CSV file with one example per row. The format for this file would be quite simple. It would be label 1, feature 1, feature 2, feature 3 and so on. If you think that you have got more data with you than Google Prediction will be able to help you with, then you can find an underlying pattern that will help you in including some other useful information as well. It all depends on the kind of information that you would want to input into the system. You have also got the option for including the word count of the text and the time as well.

The fourth step is to upload the same data into the Cloud storage provided by Google. Once you have made the data available in CSV format, then you will simply have to upload it to Google Cloud. There are different ways in which you can do this. You can make use of the web interface and access the platform with the help of a line command, or by directly using the Cloud Storage API.

The fifth step is the training of the model with the help of Google Prediction API. You can even make use of a client library for training your model. Make predictions in your applications. Now that you have managed to build a model, it is time to start making predictions. The output labels will need to be classified so that sentiment analysis is carried on in a proper manner.

The final step is for you to update your model with all the data you have. You can keep on improving your model by adding in more examples. There are two ways in which you can keep on adding additional information to the existing model. You can add additional data to the original file and then insert the same into it. You can also make use of the existing model and simply keep updating it whenever you feel like adding in more information.

Chapter 10:
Social Network Analysis

Social network analysis consists of the mapping, as well as the measuring of, the relationships and flows that exist between people, groups, organizations and various other information processing units. This method of analysis will help you in visualizing your audience and the connection that will lead you to identify the best possible manner in which you can share your knowledge.

Network mapping is an associated practice to this. This is made use of for visualizing relationships that exist within as well as outside an organization. It is used for facilitating the identification of individuals who play a key role in influencing others like leaders, politicians, experts and so on, identifying individuals or teams that are acting as bottlenecks in the flow of knowledge and the ways in which the flow of knowledge can be improved. It will help in accelerating the flow of knowledge as well as information across the organizational boundaries. This helps in improving the efficiency of the formal and the informal channels of communication that exist in an organization and also creates awareness about the importance of the informal means of networking.

Social network analysis will help in enabling a relationship between the people who provide information and then the ones that seek the same. Who do people look up to for information? Who do they share this information with? Unlike a formal organizational structure of communication that shows in detail the hierarchy of communication that is followed in management, social network analysis instead focuses on the informal relationships that exist. This will allow the managers to understand the different dynamics that exist within an organizational structure. These relationships aren't usually visible, and Social network analysis helps in displaying the same. There are real networks of communications under the skeletal structure of formal communication.

The process of this form of data analysis usually involves the usage of questionnaires or even interviews, or a combination of the two for gathering the necessary information about the different relationships that define a group. The responses that are gathered can then be made use of for further analysis. Gathering this data and then analyzing the same with help you in coming up with a baseline against which you can develop all your other plans. Priorities of the business might also change if they are being used in a proper manner. Social media is a powerful tool and you should make the most of it for the benefit of your venture.

The different stages in the process of social network analysis are mentioned in this section. It will start out with the identification of the network of people who need to be analyzed. This could be a team, a particular department or a handful of individuals. The next thing that you will need to do would be to gather all the necessary background information. You can interview various managers and even key staff members to help in understanding the different needs and problems they might have. Clarifying the objectives of the analysis and then defining its scope will help in making it more effective.

Then you will have to start formulating different questions. Make use of the survey method and design a questionnaire. Start surveying the individuals within this network and identify the various relationships that exist and the flow of information between these people. Make use of the software for visually mapping out the informal network. Review this map for identifying the various problems and opportunities that this would provide you with. Design and implement such actions that will bring about the desired outcome. Start mapping the same network after a few months to see if anything has changed.

For highlighting the importance of social networks, it is essential to create an informal map. You can do so by making use of Post-it notes and a large sheet of paper or cardboard. Ask all the participants to write their names on the notes and then put these up on the map. Ask them to then draw lines to link themselves to people they know. The second step would be to ask them to write down the name of the person who happens to be their key source of knowledge. Let them add this to the map. This will help the management in establishing the informal lines of communication and knowledge flow that exist within an organization.

Social network marketing is the new concept on the block. Facebook is worth billions of dollars and there are billions of active users on it. This is the best platform that is available for the promotion of anything. Social network analysis can be made use of for improving the marketing prospects of the business. In an industry that has always been obsessed with numbers, social network analysis is one tool that hasn't gained much popularity. However, all this was in the past. In today's world, social network analysis is as important as any other tool of data analytics. There are several practical applications of social network analysis. Businesses can make use of this for improving the flow of communication within their organization. Law enforcement can also make use of it for identifying any criminal or terrorist activities online. It can also help businesses in reaching their potential customers.

Network operators can make use of this for the optimization of their structure and also the capacity of the networks that they have.

Are there any specific businesses that can benefit from this particular tool? Well, theoretically there are no specifics. Any business or industry can benefit from this. You can make use of social network analysis for improving your sales. The aim of social network analysis is to simply reduce the viral effect that might be there in the business when the customer decides to either leave or make a purchase.

For collecting the necessary information you need, you will simply have to find the source of the informal networks, and by identifying these, you will be able to make the most of the information provided. Social network analysis can be conducted at any point in time. You can even make this a part of the other data analytics that your business might be making use of regularly.

Chapter 11:
Real-life Examples

In this chapter, let us take a look at the different real life instances where companies and businesses have made use of various tools of data analytics for improving their efficiency in operations and also for improving their profitability.

AccuWeather

How many times do you think about the weather in a day? Everyone keeps talking about the weather, don't they? However, AccuWeather does do something about it. This company helps in obtaining and then providing real-time information and news about the weather to over a million people across the globe. It does so through its website and mobile application. In the year 2015, ForecastWatch had ranked AccuWeather as a number one company for providing users with accurate forecasts regarding the weather. Most of the Android enabled devices to show the weather forecast, and this information that they provide is via AccuWeather. So, it is natural that people trust this information.

Providing information about the weather shouldn't just be about the basic climatic conditions. To set themselves apart from all their competitors, AccuWeather had to do something a little more. To provide additional value and for boosting their revenue, they tried to get a better understanding of the weather needs of their visitors of the website thus supplying the same when AccuWeather tied up with DoubleClick for Publishers (popularly known as DFP) account with Google Analytics.

AccuWeather makes use of DFP for managing and serving ads across the whole website and Google Analytics 360 with help in understanding the user behavior on the website. Before the integration of these two systems, AccuWeather wasn't able to see how this data was being intersected or the behavior of the different website visitors had been affecting its revenue. When these two platforms were linked together, the team at AccuWeather was able to get its hands on important numbers for further analysis quite quickly.

Over 1.5 billion people tend to rely on AccuWeather on a daily basis and it helps them to plan their days and protect their business interests as well. AccuWeather also provides minute-to-minute update regarding the weather conditions on any device that can support their app or open the website in a browser. The team at AccuWeather started concentrating on the user analytics that could be derived per page and for every session. The users who visit these pages tend to have certain routines that they stick to. There are some who visit the website, some who keep checking the app for any hourly updates and others who check the forecast for the next day. Once they managed to tie their revenue to these different routines, they managed to discover certain patterns that helped them and their clients as well. They understood that some pages had a higher value than the other pages and decided that they should maximize the revenue they could obtain from such sessions. The team at AccuWeather also noticed that certain routines seemed to have a higher value even though the individual pages and behaviors are both considerably less.

AccuWeather had also decided to take advantage of the unique advertising opportunities available to them. When the company managed to integrate both the accounts at DFP with Google Analytics 360, it provided them with an insight that was quite regressing to the team. They noticed that the combined reviewing they got from their customers had increased by 45% after they had integrated the accounts on both platforms and the two companies started to advertise on their main website. This increase was because of the increase in the number of users who were looking at weather updates at different exotic locations like Turkey and Barbados. The team made use of these insights and came up with tailored advertising packages that targeted these segments of the audience.

The integration of the two companies, DFP and Analytics 360 helped AccuWeather in multiple ways. For instance, one of the advertisers on this site, who was the seller of a health-related consumer product, had expressed his interest in conducting a survey regarding the users who notice his ads on this website. The integration of these two platforms helped in creating a custom audience base and the provision of appropriate information to such audience. Through the DFP account, it shared this information with the audience and the survey was then delivered to the concerned audience. In this manner, the advertiser had learned that the users who saw his ad on AccuWeather were 6.5 times as likely to make a purchase of the product within a month when compared to the users on any other site.

The perfect combination of DFP and Google Analytics 360 gave AccuWeather a better understanding of the needs of its users and the different ways in which their needs could be matched with other specific advertisers. Not just the team at AccuWeather would benefit from it, but the users would have a better experience as well. AccuWeather is now making use of behavior-based ad products, and they claim that their advertisers are reviewing it warmly. Making use of data analytics has helped in improving the business opportunities of this company.

Lenovo

Lenovo is considered to be a leading manufacturer of laptops and computers. It serves customers across the globe in over 160 countries. This is a Fortune 500 company and has always come up with innovative products that are quite diverse and it has a business model that is effective and efficient, as well as diverse to suit the global needs. The deducting of this company to strive for excellence motivated it to take up or adapt to the latest trends in marketing. The data-driven analysis helped Lenovo in identifying new growth patterns in the super competitive market of consumer electronics.

A rule-based model for measurement let owners of multiple channels claim credit for their sales. Each channel would get to report its sales as a separate report, and the channel managers analyzed all these conversions against their activity and channel metrics. This caused an inflation of the actual sales results thereby, making it extremely difficult for giving credit to the one aspect of marketing that probably helped in the improvement of sales.

Lenovo also had to overcome a huge blind spot regarding who was purchasing what. Lenovo not only sells PCs and laptops, but it also sells cell phones and tablets. For driving or increasing repeat purchases, Lenovo would have had to reach all their existing customers. Instead of following their old marketing models, the heads of marketing at Lenovo decided to let the data speak for itself by making use of an analytical platform referred to as Google Analytics 360. They wanted the data to show them the performance of the marketing program and processes as a whole, optimizing the spending across and within the channels, and looking at the best way in which the marketing budgets could be allocated for improving sales.

Within a period of about six months, Google Attribution a part of Google Analytics had delivered a completely different appraisal of the marketing performance. With the help of the existing data from the systems, the website analytics and the ad servers, all the sales were analyzed once again with the help of cross-channel fractional credit. Once this was done, the real picture of sales was reflected. The team realized the importance of awareness even for a strong brand like Lenovo.

Direct navigation and organic search were the maximum providers of the overall revenue. The marketing mix is a vital component of a good sales strategy. It is important to make sure that multiple channels are being used for the sake of marketing. Comparison shop engines also help in increasing the sales. It is not just the closers and the funnel stage analysis that was performed that provided a few surprises regarding the different channels that tend to act as closers. This helped Lenovo realize that for better sales they would have to adopt a more holistic approach and concentrate on developing and maintaining awareness of their brand and increase the influx of funds into cross-channel investments for improving sales. By analyzing the existing data and the stored data, new patterns of relationships between sales and various other components were discovered. Data helped in obtaining the actual sales projection without duplication of information.

Dominos

One of the most well-known pizza delivery services is Domino's, and it does dominate pizza sales around the world. The presence of Domino's can be found almost everywhere around the world. From the UK to Switzerland and every other country in between, the sales of this fast food chain keep on growing. In the year 2014, according to research conducted, it was proved that in Europe, it had managed to sell a staggering number of 76 million pizzas and had a turnover of about £766.7 million.

Domino's is quite the digital innovator. Most of the success of this chain can be attributed to strong e-commerce investments in platforms that would help people in purchasing pizzas quite easily. The first pizza sold online by Domino's was in the year 1999. The iPhone app of Domino's was related in the year 2010, and the Android version was quickly released after this. By the ending of 2014, customers of Domino's could also order their pizzas via their Xboxes. The marketing team at Domino's had managed to assemble various tools that would help them in measuring their performance and keeping in sync with the various innovations that were taking place. However, dealing only with information that was stored in the past hampered the ability of the marketing team for gaining the much-required insight into the actual working of the tools. The Domino's team was well aware of the value of the data insights that they were simply waiting to get their hands on. For achieving success, the team was well aware that they would need to include more than the data stored in silos, connect various data sets and also manage to gain a reporting view that was holistic.

Domino's is a leading pizza delivery chain with its headquarters situated in England. Domino's has got the simple goal of integrating their market across various devices, being able to create a view of customer behavior that is holistic and making use of a cross-channel analysis of marketing performance. They make use of various data analytics tools like Google Analytics 360, Google Tag Manager, Google BigQuery and other integrated sources of big data.

By making use of these tools of data analysis, they noticed an immediate increase in their monthly revenue by 6%, managed to save about 80% of their year over year costs of operations, increased the agility of tag management and were also privy to powerful reporting dashboards that allowed for customization. By taking a few strategic steps in collaboration with a reseller of Google Analytics, referred to as DBi, Domino's has managed to use Analytics 360 for turning their organizational goals into a daily-based reality. DBi helped in leveraging the power for data layering, for storing written code and then sending the same to Tag Manager 360. Domino's has managed to scale new heights and make the most of the situation that it is in by utilizing the different techniques of data analytics.

There are so many other companies across the world that make use of various forms of data analytical tools. Being aware of the patterns that exist in the humongous amounts of data and analyzing the past patterns will help in creating answers and taking sound management decisions. Analytics is a highly vital component of business.

Conclusion

I would like to thank you once again for purchasing this book.

There are three major sections in this book and each chapter will help you in gaining a better understanding of data analytics. The first section covers the basic information that you will need for getting started with data analytics and the different types of analytics that exist. The second part comprises of the various advantages and opportunities that data analytics will provide your business. The third section comprises of the different techniques of data analytics. There are seven major methods, and each of these techniques has various advantages and disadvantages of their own, and their viability would depend upon the reason for their use. Data analytics is a vital component if you want to achieve success. Make use of these tools in a smart way for taking better decisions and moving your business towards success.

Getting the hang of the different techniques will help you in finding the perfect tool for analyzing data that will help you in taking informed decisions. You will no longer feel confused when you are discussing any future business plans that involve the analysis of data, and you will find this easier to understand. It is important that you have a basic knowledge of all these various concepts so that you can take the most profitable decisions for your business. By now, you should have realized that data analytics is not as intimidating as it would seem on the surface. All it requires is a little time and patience. Then you will simply need to start applying this theoretical information to your daily business operations in order to get the hang of it.

Thank you once again. I hope the book will help you in your journey to make your business flourish!

www.ingramcontent.com/pod-product-compliance
Lightning Source LLC
Chambersburg PA
CBHW060941050326
40689CB00012B/2539